POETRY VIRGINIA 2024

1923
2023

Collected Winning Poems
Annual Contest Awards
Poetry Society of Virginia

HighTide
Publications, Inc.
DELTAVILLE, VA

First Edition 2024

Published by High Tide Publications, Inc.
Deltaville, Virginia
https://www.HighTidePublications.com

Graphic Arts: Firebelliedfrog.com

Printed in the United States of America.

The Poetry Society of Virginia is the state's oldest poetry nonprofit. The organization was founded in May 1923 in Williamsburg. We encourage excellence in writing, reading, study, and the appreciation of poetry through annual poetry contests, an annual anthology, book awards, statewide readings and programs, and literary festivals.

This is the annual anthology for 2024, featuring 54 first and second place poems from 27 adult contest categories. (We also offer an annual student contest, this year with 16 categories, open to students from lower school to 12th grade, but those winning poems do not appear here.)

While for some adult categories only society members are eligible to enter, anyone who wishes to join the society, nationally or internationally, may do so, and most categories are open to all, regardless of membership status, upon payment of an entrance fee. **Submissions close each year on Edgar Allan Poe's birthday, January 19**. Entries are submitted via submittable.com; each category is judged blind by a different judge. Up to four prizes may be awarded per category; the top two in each category are offered publication. Visit https://www.poetrysocietyofvirginia.org/ in the late fall to see the requirements and opportunities for our 2025 contests.

Derek Kannemeyer, Editor

POETRY SOCIETY OF VIRGINIA
CONTEST CATEGORIES AND HONOREES
2024

1. EDGAR ALLAN POE MEMORIAL: Wendell Hawken, Judge
   Any form. Any subject. No line limit.

2. SARAH LOCKWOOD MEMORIAL: Bart White, Judge
   Sonnet in rhyme and meter. Any subject.

3. BESS GRESHAM MEMORIAL: Kim Hazelwood, Judge
   Any form. On friends and friendship.

4. CARLETON DREWRY MEMORIAL: Nicole Yurcaba, Judge
   Any form. On farm life or working the earth.

5. BRODIE HERNDON MEMORIAL: Angela Carter, Judge
   Any form. Subject: heroism.

ADULT WINNERS
1ST AND 2ND PLACE

1923

2023

1ˢᵗ - Erin Newton Wells: *Ex Machina*

It began one day when Dante, not the man
but the dog, lay down in the street to sleep.

His age inspired it, the street as good as any
when warmth like this was needed, sleep

ever more longed for in his dog years, equal,
we are told, to at least ninety of ours. Sleep

came quickly, the sun gently drawing up its
welcome blanket on him, and in that sleep

he dreamed of enormous meadows, though
not by that word. What dogs call it. Sleep

became delicious with every scent in which
a dog's nose finds quivering joy, such sleep

as gave access to all he desired, no need to
beg for it, and he romped as if new. Sleep,

like this, he could regard as something holy,
although, of course, no word for it. Sleep

came, *the love that moves the sun and stars*,
mainly sun, for stars are hard to feel. Sleep

came with its long promise, *as a wheel turns
smoothly, free from jars.* Dear sudden sleep,

a woman kneeling, weeping like a mother
at his silence, car mid-street. Blessed sleep.

(Paradiso, Canto 33)

2nd - Hannah Rouse: *night-time skincare*

I.   melting balm

wash satin finish stains   from your face   the water
so scalding   so   scathing   it boils you   alive   while
brewing in the breathlessness   of obsession   you   realize
somehow you're eager   to grow up but afraid
                    to age
expiration haunts   you   yet still   you're willing   to die
                              wishing   for the space
provided with maturity
he'll   want you   only   if you're
    old enough to love but
young enough to be desired   fresh
                         forgiving

II.   foaming face wash

in this bathroom   you watch yourself   barren   exposed
                    speckled scarlet cheeks staring back at you
without heat   without the pleasure of him   in past tense
          you are unable to breathe   articulate
                    your thoughts or   your fingers
    your skin the texture   of clementines
you tell yourself
maybe   it's just the smell   tangy   tangerine-crusted
          something akin to smoke
making you believe   you're made of plastic
          you hope he sees you   shimmering   on display
     begging   waiting   for
him to prove you wrong

III.   toner

every night you search   in all the blue   blurry glass bottles
of products   with names you can't pronounce   for proof that
          the beauty broadcasted on your phone screen is   real
     evidence of something   lovable   living between   your limbs
               you look for signs
     of glamor   worthiness
          but there's so much
                    cheap toner   still   aching
                    in your eyes
you can't see anything

IV.   hyaluronic acid

to say he groomed you   would be to   admit that
          he &
          all your glass bottles lied
you're not   special
                    sexy
                        starstruck   sun kissed
nothing about you   reeks   of radiance
          the meteor shower of a married man
was not love   clandestine   & fated
          you were   burned   boiled
          you were   led   one frightful footstep
                    after another
into the forest fire   of his arms

V.   aloe facial spray

sometimes when you think about   him   talking
to your reflection in the foggy mirror   as if he's standing
                    in front of you   your chest tightens
          so sharp you think your ribs will scrape
against one another   &   you keep   loving
                                                    living
addicted to the smell of his apologies
                        his touch   one fabled
          finger at a time   seeing you

VI.   eye cream

you picture him on his deathbed: body long
having betrayed him   memory   lost
    to music   madness   marriage
                              eyes   sunken in
skin hanging   loose   loveless
labyrinthian veins lit by longing
                    stories sketched
in   the palms   of his hollow hands
                              all the girls
                              the ghosts
          the glass   the gasoline   &
the grime of   gentleness
beating   breaking   like his   bones

VII. *moisturizer*

in moments like these   skin dewy   dusk-soaked
        you wonder   how much longer   you have
    until   you are no longer   limitless
    until   you are singing   to the burnt leaves
                    wrapping   yourself in the wreckage   for comfort
your expiration date   is not plastered on your breasts
the way you often think it is   but buried   between
your thighs   a whisper on   your dripping lips: *this body*
will break down &   how
will you be   beautiful then?

VIII. *hydrating lip mask*

you know   *teenage dream* has to   end
        one day
you know   you   will   grow
        out of glitter   lip gloss   giggles
        removed from the   glow of   girlhood
you know   you'll learn to live without   the luxury of protection
                    & you think
you know the scent   taste   earnestness
        of heartbreak   but
    it only   lingers   long
                enough to   sting
        & he will not be around to mourn
        the youth he stole from you

1ˢᵗ - toni tyler: *Skin*

Our choices change with matching smiles or frowns.
Our friendship strains from finding ways to cope
With voices musing who wears pants or gowns.
Our kinship pains to mingle touch with grope.
Our longings watch as others try to judge
When closeness seems to agitate their fears.
Our hanging nears when hate just needs a nudge
Or happens if we fail to gain their ears.
Our difference may now belie their law
Which of itself denies our freeborn path.
Our precedence besets to spy their flaw
While in itself ignores their zealot wrath.

I now propose each me become our we
Then let our children show one skin to see.

2ⁿᵈ - Wendell Hawken: *Diapause*

Here come the wobbly days of milk-rimmed mouths.
And buzz. A few songbirds have joined the crows.
Smell the warm. Barn swallows, some three weeks south,
but coming. He's finished his first harrow.
Soon our ladybugs will stir, leave their corner
of our kitchen where they wait out winter
every year, six or seven huddled up
above us tucked in lamplight on the couch.
A fire. His legs laid across my lap.
They will dissolve into the season, much
like him in spring days' grease and gasoline,
the hum past dark of farm machines.
Glancing up from shelling peas, I will see
my mind's mirage of cold's past company.

1st - Christina Linsin: *Bikes*

for Nea

 Bright fuchsia socks under dark blue jelly shoes, sidewalk pine needles slick under feet balanced on both sides of dense rubber tires, temporarily pinioned beneath splattered splash guards, like cartographers recording past adventures. Ghosts of an earlier ride clacked a set of spoke beads once, and then they rested silent. Long dark hair leaned like language from soft mouths, just wanting me to understand how it was. "She's my friend, really, so if you're going to play here, you'll have to play with me too." The blessing of certainty. I liked her immediately.

"Alright," assenting easily, "Wha'd'ya wanna do?" Sweaty breezes filtered through long hallways of dense green boughs, carrying the scent of camphor – a prickly journey, earthy and cool.

"Trampoline?"

I had a trampoline. Well, my older sister did, anyway. Same thing in this case. "What else were you thinking?" Melodies of songbirds beckoned. It was a sacred Saturday in deep August. The first Saturday after school had opened its greedy jaws and gulped down the last dregs of summertime adventures.

The morning light reflected in eyes exactly the color of the pine needles on which she stood. "Bikes?"

I smiled into forever. "I was hoping you'd say that."

2nd - Wes Carrington: *Perfect Poems*

"Find and share the perfect poems." –poets.org

In perfect poems, you open the door wide
welcoming in the long-lost friend
with a big smile and a hug.
You sit and chat, no agenda, no hurry,
just two old friends catching up
over cups of coffee, or something stronger.

Maybe it's that high school friend
you traded confidences with
as darkness faded and the sun rose
with such pink promise after the prom.
Everyone else had gone home and
you talked about how the future
stretched out, like railroad tracks
running side-by-side to the horizon
until they merged at the point
where they vanished.

Maybe it's that college buddy
with whom you spent intense months
navigating foreign lands and languages,
eating your way through Europe:
ice cream in Moscow, *croque monsieurs*
in Paris, tapas in Madrid. You bonded
over the adventure of it all, but lost touch
afterwards building a career,
raising a family, living a life:
the sameness of it all.

Maybe it's that friend from work
who labored beside you in those
cubicles-called-offices as you
rose in bureaucratic ranks,
or not; who brightened those tiresome
days with a smile and a
did you hear the one about?
and you realized only after he was gone
that no workplace should be without
sharing and trust.

The hours pass, drinks are drained
and refilled, evening comes and
curtains are drawn to keep the night away
but finally, it's time to go. On the porch
you turn back hoping to whisper
an iambic reminder of why friends
are important in our lives but—unlike in
perfect poems—now the verses catch in your throat.
Maybe it's the cold, or something else you think,
as the taillights, and words, fade away.

1ˢᵗ - Gail Giewont: *Dianthus*

Seeds black like dead stars
blend into the earth
and refuse to grow.

In the spring, they rise up
in clusters, every year
fewer, a war their roots
seem to be losing.

I want to be a good gardener.
I want to perpetuate
this space with blossoms,
take scissors to the seed pods after
the flowers have gone brown.
Seeds I hope to plant later clatter
into a plastic bag. I snip until
a plump round body tumbles
dark as a grape from the leaves,
a red spot on its belly.

There is danger in what I want to nourish.

I am a bad gardener. I cannot stop the dianthus
from dying. The weeds take over,
crowding into the space where something else
is meant to bloom. Maybe it is the weeds
that should live.

2nd - A Logan Hill: *When it is time*

When it is time
to take over my father's rituals
of getting drunk
and mowing the lawn
or stacking the wood
behind the woodshed
or dumping the gathered grass
into the creek
or teaching small children
what they are told
they need to know
or showing my son how to
change the oil
or where to get the best
barbecue chicken on
Saturday mornings
or how to make a pie
or cook a steak
or to make a kite out of
twigs from the fallen
branches
or to file my taxes
or find a wife
to get a job
or to fall asleep in the
stale heat of a
summer afternoon
eating popsicles
there comes with it the
ownership of my home.

Before Mr. Breneman came to the valley
and built the brownstone that I live in
there were people who did not know the
meaning of the word.

Before the walls were painted over
and covered up again with faint wallpaper
the men wrote love poems to women.

Before the trees and the streams
and the loud noise of tractors

Before the highway came through there were
plentiful rolling fields that my grandfather owned
and worked down with his bare hands.

There was a town and a single road,
one creek, one store

and in the pool hall behind the store
my father and his father
would eat large cheeses
from the counter.

1st - Joseph M. Jablonski: *A Poem about Dragons for My Son*

Someone left the cave
Open
To our pasts.

They roost in there,
Inside those eaves doors
Of the mind
You may want to fear.

Scaly, weird,
Sometimes appear
During arguments.

Your mother and I,
We will deny,
Yes, we will lie.

So, I gave you that child's book
About such things as dragons.

And also this poem,
Shaped like a sword,
Knighting thee with
Responsibility

To find these creatures,
To admit they are real.

Because when they crawl
From the skeletons
In our attics

They are hunting your soul -
Clawing at missing Truth
To breathe fire in
Flaws to grow.

And we all have flaws.
We all have claws.

Because, yes,
You will deny,
You will lie
Too.

We all stuff our dragons
Into attics.

But some like to ignore,
Prefer not to lift
This heavy sword.

But this sword, don't you see?

Don't you see you must
Slay your flawed humanity

To really be a hero?

2nd - Peter LaBerge: *Homosexual Panic*

David Self, 1985

I imagine the night another way: knife through the laminate cover of a bible in a bleached kitchen sink. Bruises where the fingers squeeze, then crush a bagged peach. Knife through a framed painting of a sleeping saint. Knife wrapped in burlap, tossed down the stone neck of a backyard well. Perhaps to slit open the starless gut of February, perhaps stowed. Perhaps your name wandering the fields, a lost firefly. David: Pendleton. David: Fort Thomas. David.

Instead, the night: neatly disemboweled as winter against the windows. Meeting at Subway Bar, then back to his place.

The night: fingers, a necklaced bruise. Larynx, a squeezed peach. A paring knife, then a cigarette butt lodged in your starless gut. A future & queer wandering the fields.

1st - Elizabeth Black: *Issa's Cricket*

he flees the grasp
of a tiny sparrow beak,
flings himself
on a splintered branch,
floating down river

tethered to this uncertain ark,
navigates
the only direction he can go—
forward adventuring
the unknown

antennae and eyes seek
to understand peril
and miracle
on coursing sways and swells
circling obstacles

chances eddies and rapids—
sometimes barely afloat
churring panic,
sometimes cruises
singing a rhapsody

sails to his final rest
on tired sedge
shadowing water
to rub failing wings
in grateful chirrups

2nd - Richard Stimac: *Ares*

When the young men entered the house, they raped
the daughters, threw the infant on the floor,
shot the son and father against the door.
And taped it all. But the mother escaped.
And testified. In court, her shaved head draped
in mourning, she uttered the truths of war.
The courtroom quiet, she told, as she swore,
how, by coincidence, our lives are shaped.
Across the water, someone scans the news,
sips green tea, and considers if a nap
is deserved today. A broken-backed book
lies open, on the bed. Thick blankets wrap
a body. A sunset of greens, reds, blues
draws attention, as if to beg a look.

1st - Erin Newton Wells: *Someone on a Journey*

(Gulnisa Iman, Uyghur poet, imprisoned 2010)

In Urumqi, in Xinjiang, museum of the Autonomous
Region, *Tocharian Woman, Human Mummy*, lies
under glass where others observe the anomaly
with different features, her blond braids, pensive face,

woman found in a tumulus whose salt sand and aridity
preserved her outward form, a stiff arm arrested
as she seems to reach an invisible thing, gone now
for centuries, flown, as words will do unless written,

flickering from the mind, lost, unless whispered,
smuggled out, as some try to do in a prison of silence,
also in Urumqi. Or call it *reeducation*, as they say.
Or call it something like a tomb where truth and poetry

are named divisive, as from this teacher, a woman
not Tocharian but different, poetry a part of how
she breathes, to be buried for it all these years. Or
Simply consider me as / someone on a journey,

she writes. *If I'm alive, at some point, I / shall return,*
a screen shot of these scribbled words passed
to someone else, destroyed, memorized, passed on,
the risk of death placed against slow desiccation,
a hand writing on the air, reaching to one who listens.

*(Title and lines quoted are from "Untitled," 2020, one of two of Iman's poems
smuggled from prison. She was falsely accused, sentenced to life, sentence reduced in
2017 to 19 years after a statement of contrition, likely forced by torture. She is held
in No. 2 Prison, Urumqi, Xinjiang Uyghur Autonomous Region.)*

2nd - April J. Asbury: *The British Tour*

She was supposed to see it with me: the yellow gorse
flaming from the hills, the white foam of hawthorn
gliding past our window, the glitter of glass
scattered on Hadrian's broken wall.

I couldn't bring her back. Couldn't unspeak
    next year
    next time
    when we feel better
    soon, soon, soon

On one cobbled street like other cobbled streets,
I slipped into a dim cathedral. When the sun flare ebbed,
I could make out stone floors, vaulted windows, beams
and pews of ancient dark wood. Under a blur of saints
stood the staid business of pamphlets, candles, a lockbox
next to rows of cards and pencil stubs. This Methodist girl
searched for a few pence, then dropped cold coins in the slot.

I lit a single candle. By its glow, I scribbled
my mother's name. I did not pray; I had nothing left,
just coins, the smell of singed wax, the wavering light
of dozens of candles. But when the wick kindled,
I didn't want to stop. I would light candles
in York, Bath, St. Paul's itself, any nave
open to let a motherless girl inside.

Even when the signs said *no, not for you,*
I wrote her name, paid my coins, added light
to the radiant cloud. Soon I burned candles
for them all: grandmother, aunts, teachers,
all the names I carried. Someone in this strange land
would see their names and know: these women
were loved, and it didn't matter if each card
were tossed casually in the trash. The candle
burned, the white wax wept, tears
kissed the stones. Light cradled
me in hallowed places
they never lived to see.

1st - Rich Follett: *crt*

white child holds black hand
lifelong love blooms in schoolyard
bullets whizzing by

2nd - Elizabeth Spencer Spragins: *Color Blind*

my sightless sister
grips the kindness in his hand—
a solid color
with warmth of sourwood honey
fills the cracks in broken days

1st - Felicity Sheehy: *First Flight*

When the nose tips up, I don't think
    of my mother. There at the departure
gate, like a woman underwater, her face
    the dark tug of a dream. Nor of my father,
off to one side, tilting his camera, already
    watching me on a screen. I don't think
of the dogs, sprawled in their sleeping beds,
    or of the fields we passed, the whole drive
down, licked clean of summer, all those apples
    I won't stay to see. In the version I'd like to tell,
I am already looking ahead, my hands not
    shaking, my mind full of this future I'd thought
I'd want. But I am small and human
    and crinkling a paper cup in my hands.
Next to me a man is tapping his flight map.
    And there are people smoothing their coats,
people reading, people talking, people snug
    in the soft ports of their headphones, far away.
I'm not thinking of them. When the nose
    tips up, I am watching the light push its way
across my window, each droplet in its darkness,
    smaller and smaller now.

2nd - Peter LaBerge: *Polari*

The Forgotten Secret Language of Gay Men
            —Slate, Manchester, 2016

Manchester—a hand pressed against a gray curtain.
            All velvet & silk. Violet sash, field mid-war. Field
in impulsive spring. Rows of wooden horses
            lining village storefronts. Nude, no reins. Whittled
from memory down to ghost. Only these boys
            left to gallop across cobblestones. Polari—the boys
in the snow-bitten field, outside town. Beauty, the ghost
            of unmet need. The bodies pinquiet. Manchester,
1967—empty mouth blooming into filled mouth. Punch
            of cherry blossom, sprig of mint. Some wooden horses
sold plainly for cash, the rest whittled by fire. The boys
            piercing the night with their ending. Could the town hear
their slow crackle in its mouth? Polari—the language
            a queer boy speaks while dying, afraid
  of what his own death will mean. As the overnight rain
            polishes even the darkest townhouses, as their god
sharpens his teeth, the cherry blossoms flit back up
            the sleeves of trees. When god called the mouths
of townspeople open, he wasn't talking about them—
            he was talking beyond them, from the field of a myth
enflamed, about petrified mouths, soundless hooves.

1st - Erin Newton Wells: *Crane, Briefly Seen*

The drawing shows a carrier pigeon, a shadow
      high in the corner, small, flying left.

Below it, in the center, full color, drawn large
      to fill the page and facing right,

is the crane stepping forward in those splendid
      white feathers, the red cap

by which we know it, and the zero yellow eye,
      a lesson meant to teach *extinct*

and *extant*, perhaps what I remember so early
      this morning close to the creek,

drawn there, called by the sound of water after
      so much rain, my vantage

from a narrow bridge, the path below cloaked
      in fog so there appears to be

this very bird on its long familiar legs, the failed
      egg hatched once more, resurrected,

flown here and given back for just this moment,
      a cloud of white, a pale smear of red

on its head, the stillness as it forms in my mind,
      hoarse whoop of its cry heard

in this unexpected place, its brief reassurance
      what is over is not over.

2nd - Wes Carrington: *An Ostentation*

*"The sight of a feather in a peacock's tail, whenever I gaze
at it, makes me sick!"* — *Charles Darwin, 1860*

Killer of snakes.
Bundle of contradictions.
I am divine. I am royal.
I am wise. I am prideful.

Hera's favorite, I'm this too—
India's national bird
and NBC's symbol of color TV.
No black & white for me!

I'm a throne on which no man sits,
and a wicker chair. I puzzled Darwin,
made him sick, my plumage
not fitting into his theory.

But Charlie, once survival's assured,
maybe selection *is* sexual.
Female's choice. Ladies' night.
A Sadie Hawkins dance.

Hey, quick fact: sixty percent of my
body length exists solely to attract.
Yes, I have to work hard to put on a show.
I rock and roll and shake my tail

feathers to find a mate, who I'm sure
will be great raising those chicks all alone.
I'm sorry, honey, but you *did* pick *me*.
A peacock. Who can fly.

1st - Kathleen P. Decker: *Shelter*

Ukraine

below-ground
in the bomb shelter
gentle strains
and quick arpeggios
rise to the street

dirt on her cheeks
dust in her hair
and occasionally
phrases are drowned out
by thunder overhead
of ceaseless artillery

sitting in rapt attention
neighbors, family, and strangers
united by fear
unified by yet another pogrom
uplifted by violin-song

despots fear freedom
they cannot chain cadenzas
and so, the bombs continue
dreams of peace
awakened by music

2nd - Donna Isaac: *With its Bright Shining*

Two horses with blinders graze behind a fence.
Blush oak holds a cawing crow.

Five geese drift across a pond.
A hooded boy casts for bass.

Thistles hide in ghostly grass.
Grey sky looms.

In morning fog, sugar pumpkins,
squash, and greens brighten an open market.

Four days ago, nurses adjusted my body
beneath radiation, photons precisely aimed.

I imagined sunlight upon my eyelids,
floating in a summer-cold pool.

Can I stand outside myself and see?
Take in the cornucopia, the barley moon?

Remember autumn drifts of gold,
standing beneath the glow?

1st - Erin Newton Wells:

Emoji, or Lament for the Written Word

Back in the paleolithic,
writing was not so prolific.
A picture or two
would just have to do,
simple and somewhat specific.

Then, why, with our relative ease
to write now whatever we please,
does that smiley face
and red heart replace
what took us so long to achieve?

2nd - Laura J. Bobrow: *The Birds and the Bees*

When a drone bee's attracted by sex to
a queen bee he wants to sleep next to,
he brings her a gift
and she soon gets the drift.
Making love's on his mind. He expects to.

If she finds that his offer is tangible,
she clutches him tight with her mandible.
That is how babies come.
Huh? Then I must be dumb,
though to bees it is quite understandable.

1st - Eric Forsbergh: *Free Speech Privilege*

Vietnam, 1972
For Colin Kaepernick

The tarmac squirms as a Da Nang sun
smothers us at dress inspection.

At attention, I'm second-left. Tall to short
makes better lines. Uniformity.

Our chief stops to eye each man.
Bullets of sweat mingle in his Afro
high and tight. He's compact as a pistol.
His effort gleams: buttons, buckle, shoes.
And on his shoulder,
Stars and Bars in heavy starch.

He halts. Point blank at me.
Locked in, he squints.
His voice downshifts for traction.

What makes you so special
you can mouth off against this war?
Do like me sailor. Shut your yap.

Now with all these years I realize what he saw:
my specific diction, my John Lennon glasses,
me in a bubble of electronic countermeasures,
my skin with no tattoos, my palms a pale putty.

But what burns at him below the surface,
barely regulation,
is my hair in sheaves of wheat,
another sign my harvest is a given.

2nd - James Huneycutt: *You Cannot Marry Roger Vadim, He's Far Too Dead*

You cannot marry Roger Vadim, he's far too dead
for you to waste your matrimonial instincts upon.
Why don't you seek out a living spouse instead?

Although you wander where the tide has led,
don't swim salmon-like upstream to spawn.
You cannot marry Roger Vadim, he's far too dead.

Among a truckload of questions that burden my head,
I'd ask, among other conclusions not already drawn,
why don't you seek out a living spouse instead?

Just because your finances are momentarily in the red
and his post-mortem residuals have only grown,
you cannot marry Roger Vadim, he's far too dead.

Though he got Bardot, Fonda, and Deneuve in bed,
probably accompanied by "Afternoon of a Fawn,"
why don't you seek out a living spouse instead?

Yes, it's true, his films were a kind of smarmy sex-ed.
Yet if directed, you'd act naked, backlit by Klieg light dawn.
You cannot marry Roger Vadim, he's far too dead.
Why don't you seek out a living spouse instead?

1st - Erin Newton Wells: *If Windows Remain*

Chambered Nautilus, by Andrew Wyeth, 1956, tempera

Whatever makes you sorrow has become
a wisp of curtain on the canopy,

the window closed. It cannot be a wind
outside but something here within the room

to stir the gauze and fringe, to cause a sigh
as though it breathes. An umber shadow drifts

around the edge, but you are clearly lit
as if by sun on sea, or by a cloud

passed by the glass. Nothing to see outside
but what you see, a vista all in white,

the sea grass flattened by the wind, no one
but you to walk between the air and sleep.

But do not sleep, not yet. The bed becomes
a ship, a shell, and luminous will rise,

its chambers delicate and filled with light,
the glow a hollowed pearl in rooms of air.

Whatever caused the pain will fall away
and pain will vanish, nothing left but wind

to sweep the house if windows still remain,
if glass is cleared, the sash is raised, and you

are free, the memories that held you down
released, and none of them can hold you here.

andrew wyeth chambered nautilus - Search Images (bing.com)

2nd - June Goodenough: *Evoked by George Sotter's A Snowy Night*

of moonlit trees no leaf to turn the wind
a path of tracks in snow to fade from sight
a flicker bright a fire to call me home
old house of stone alone all warm it sits
so snug a night the thought of cold is gone

oil on canvas, 1939, Philadelphia Museum of Art
https://philamuseum.org/collection/object/303956

1st - Greg Friedmann: *No Deus, No Machina*

The great heron stands, immobile, on the riverbank,
not fishing in the green water at the shoreline

but midway up the bank, staring at the ground.
Herons can live fifteen years or more, so his

may be the shadow I've seen rising from the river
these many years as he's taken wing; his croak

the voice I've heard scolding my many intrusions.
He remains still all day, head tucked under wing:

dying. He waits for dusk and looming rain,
his last meager hope for camouflage

against the fox making his nightly maraud.
He, the fox, and I: each helpless to change

this denouement — no Deus, no machina.
I imagine both sets of eyes, locking in twilight:

one pair suddenly agleam at nature's boon,
jaws thirsty for that long, thin neck;

but in the heron's eyes, what? Fear? Acceptance?
Gently at first, then harder, the rain falls.

2ⁿᵈ - Sarah E N Kohrs: *Sieved with Galium Aparine*

*"I am dying," written by buffalo-hunter Phillip Vetter in his own
blood after a grizzly bear attack by Greybull River, Wyoming, 1892*

Chicory roasted by the fire.
Silver-scaled salmon
sizzled in a pan of oil
before bruised herbs
consecrated a final meal.

I wonder if a pail, hat, and rifle
were what he last expected to hold
in a land that saw the collision
of how people lived. With nebulous
boundaries, river-locked or denoted

by the grandeur of a tree,
now gone. With peace pines
chopped for cabins and sacred
sites mined of precious ores.
With buffalo carcasses

settled like cicada skins,
in the end. How many did you kill?
How many must I make amends
for, while you rest in Old Town?
Both heart-crushed and pining

for something lost. We are furled
to a future that we often forget
will be. Steeped, as we are, only
in last days talk, instead of tending to
a meal cooked for friends by the water.

How do I live harmoniously
to what thrives wildly without
me? What words will I weave
into a death song the wind
sieves with *Galium aparine*?

1st - Sarah E N Kohrs: *A New Home: One Woman's Belief in Ambience*

"The gentle hunter, having pursued and tamed her quarry, crossed over to a new home"- epitaph for Alice Catherine Evans (1881-1975)

Gleaned from a spleen
under a first quarter moon,
brucellae undulate even
in breathy wisps noticed
when the world is cold.

How many died from
the unseen? Savoring
minutes-old milk straight
from the teat and settled
with froth at the table?

Zoonotic sheen glistening.
Devouring what malingers.
Yet, heated into ambience,
tamed brucellae no longer
miscarry what women

know in a world of men.
No longer ache like a mild
break from childhood games
under a first quarter moon
when the world was cold.

2nd - Anna Isabella Fratarcangelo: *Beauty Breaking Bad*

After "Snow White the Scientist" by Sarah Maple, 2011

Miss Snow,
daughter of Walter and
chef to the dwarfed dealers.
She has an aptitude for
manufacturing narcotics,
particularly producing
psychostimulants.
However,
methamphetamine
synthesis isn't as easy
as one may think.
Clandestine chemistry
has many risks, even if
you're professionally trained.
Respecting the Nagai method,
she uses pseudoephedrine as a
precursor. From then on,
she just follows
the recipe.
Her workstation is
littered with coffee filters,
matchbooks, road flares,
iodine tinctures,
blister packs of
over-the-counter cold
medicine, and Mason jars
filled with unidentifiable
solvents.
She takes care
not to die in an ignition
of ice, but she doesn't feel
alive. The best she can make
of the boys' club known as her
profession is to go back into
the kitchen and cook for
a hopeless junkie.

Still, she
has no woodland
creatures coming to
help pay off her tuition.
So, she must abandon her
snowy silk gloves, snap the blue
latex onto her dainty hands,
replace her tiara with safety
goggles, and roll up the hem
of her dress to avoid
creating a lab
hazard.

https://collection.museum.virginia.edu/objects-1/info/19673

1st - Donna Isaac: *Coming Home*

As a shoe salesman he drove many miles
in a station wagon, left arm crooked
out the window, a glimpse of gold watch,
farmer's tan. His fingers tapped a country tune.

In the back, he hauled sample cases
with snaps along with a paper bag
packed with a ham sandwich, an apple,
two homemade cookies.

He'd go up into the mountains,
small towns that still had general stores,
mercantile shops, or ancient downtown
department stores, like Leggett's or Nachman's.

Sometimes Mama set out a plate
in case he made it home.
It was cleared away after
a casserole or soup.

If he kept going, he'd be home late
sometimes bringing sausage and onion pizza.
We kids smelled it from our bedrooms
and came sniffing down the stairs.

My father has been long gone now,
52 years since the late-night crash.

Yesterday I waited at a red light
and saw a man's arm hanging out
his window, elbow bent, wristwatch on,
and wondered:

>   Who has set a place for him?
>   Who is waiting up?

2nd - Amasa Maleski: *Catch and Release*

Dad is in the boat, silent—teaching me to be silent.
The worms grow ridges on their skin when they writhe,
their anguish pricking my small heart.
Dad shrugs it off. He has to bait the hook for me sometimes.

When he explained that short little tug after the bite
as he mimed it going through his lip
I asked, "doesn't that hurt"
he said, "probably—"
but we always release.

One time, he caught a turtle by accident.
With the unflinching care of a surgeon
he took the spear out of the creature's face
and placed it back, *plunk*, into the lake.
       "will he be okay?"
                      "probably."

My dad is sometimes a fish.
We breathe the same love
but his heart has gills, so sometimes
his love comes out bubbles to me.
It seems there are invisible hooks
in his vertebrae and belly and heart.
       "doesn't that hurt?" I ask.
He shrugs and
            releases.

1st - Anna Evas: *A Modern Venus of Willendorf*

Benefits Supervisor Sleeping, Lucian Freud, 1995

Gorgeous fat stuffed
in a love seat of puce roses —
sponge cake arm,

pudding breast,
custard belly with
raisin garnish,

derrière a round of brie,
thighs buttered, foot
a braided challah —

you, woman,
are the soul alfresco,
bulwark against

the hard things.

https://en.wikipedia.org/wiki/Benefits_Supervisor_Sleeping

2nd - Erin Newton Wells: *Still Life*

Winter Fields, by Andrew Wyeth, 1942, tempera on composition board, Whitney Museum of American Art

A long lens of cloud lies across the sky,
a washed-out sky,
the cloud blue-gray with all of winter in it.

Below, so small, distant, difficult to see,
a dim line of trees,
two with bare arms held to the sky.

Then, what must be a house and barn,
not more than lumps
that far away, and with no warmth in them.

Both could fit into the head of a bird,
this one, near, large enough
against a narrow field, dark wings folded.

Sky, tree, house, field, a dream of a bird.
Or no dream at all.
It is done, frozen. The eye cannot see.

The head is partly hidden by dry grass,
a spray of it, pale and thinned
of its better season, the ground too cold.

And, here, just beyond its stiff gray feet,
tissue pods of lantern
each hang empty of its one red seed.

wyeth winter fields - Search Images (bing.com)

1st - James Huneycutt: *The Bats of Rabat*

Was it your fate to evict a bat tonight?
Was a tar roof where you sat tonight?

Those fluttering about your property
Enjoy a feast of insects. Eat tonight!

Young pups cling close to mother's warmth.
Together they fly as a two-headed rat tonight.

Consider, if you will, their echolocation:
ultrasonic insect combat tonight.

Nature has sharpened harmonious ears.
Bats can detect the tiniest gnat tonight.

Shaking on a ladder, stubborn as my rafter bat,
I've got an overdue eviction to work at tonight.

Fighting acrophobia with kif, trying not to go splat tonight.
Higher than Icarus; high as Paul Bowles in Rabat tonight.

2nd - Ken Hines: *Obit Postscript*

The good news is, his tinnitus
    lived on. When that day came,
        it hovered above his urn and

the white lilies his sister brought to
    the funeral—like an invisible bee.
        Visitors in their woeful clothes

huddled by the claret drapes and heard
    nothing. But it was there. Unflinching,
        standing watch. The sole part of him

death left unchanged. Did he ever
    actually listen to it? Notice how it labored
        in his inmost part? His Self's self?

How it stayed up late to hiss in his ear
    when the day's grating noise was gone.
        And treating his snores as a sort of

reply, it kept whispering in its strange
    wordless tongue, steadfast as a mother's
        love, content to have him to itself, at last.

1st - Mark Fryburg: *Dunes*

Millennia ago, the sand blew in to dam the estuaries as the ice age warmed and the water rose to become a precious lake playground of our youth where we lay exhausted on the dunes at night while a kind breeze cleared the ocean mist. We gazed at a billion stars, us, splendidly humbled by God's cathedral ceiling, still naively believing, barely noticing the dune moved under us, reclaiming its creation, a slow avalanche pressed by new dark winds in elliptical waves—taking our lake as prize, smothering with grit our last residue, innocence. Men who held our hope for America murdered; our schoolmates marching off to lose their humanity in Asian jungles. Each of us carried a wallet card stamped: "You're Next."

2nd - Peter LaBerge: *California Avenue*

Palo Alto, California

Boys are calling the hotline just before midnight again,
naked in the white-wicker mouths of bedroom closets.
They are paying out of pocket for the emergency tests.

They wanted the evening until they were full of what
it became. And you are seeding them again, seeding
elegies inside of them. Knowing they will pincushion

inside the urgent care's halogen as you uncork another.
They may not trust any man for years, even themselves
who, in their fogged bathroom mirrors, watch

as the shower fills space with thought. Especially
themselves. The doctor strung your elegy out
first thing Friday morning, let the blood and promised

he would call Tuesday, maybe Monday. He fed me
a rattling pill-bottle cap, filled a paper bag
for twenty-eight days. *Queer penance*, I joked outside

to the palms frocking the bus stop. But it wasn't
penance—it wasn't even queer. It was surviving
your vanishing condom, your vanishing

test results, one lie after the next. It was peaceful—almost
beautiful—your low house with its rhododendrons
oblivious to one side, orange blossoms shuddering

the highway below. No cars but a white panel
bakery truck. Does the yard's streetlight still shine
that bed new-penny copper each night? Do moths

gather and lick in memory? Do you ever think to check?

1st - Patsy Asuncion: *Habits of American Habitat*

I do many small things just to change my habits…
– Greta Thunberg, Environmental Activist

When I drink my water from a handy plastic bottle   or from a glass at home,
use store retail and grocery bags   or my own recyclable containers,
buy cheap picnic utensils and supplies   or use my home provisions,
    I add to the more than 5.25 trillion pieces of ocean plastic,
    250 million metric tons by 2025   or not.

When I drink my convenient K-Cup coffee   or brew in a coffeepot,
stop at a fast-food place for take-out   or bring my brown bag lunch,
buy a frozen, prepackaged meal   or make a simple dish at home,
    I add to the 268 million tons of US garbage   #1 in world
    in toxic landfills or polluting incinerators   or not.

When I grasp a paper towel to swipe a spill   or cloth rag to clean a spot,
buy eggs in Styrofoam containers   or get fruit in eco-friendly bags,
cover lunch in plastic wrap   or store leftovers in old glass jars,
    I add to *un*recylables in toxic landfills, or worse,
    the *25% already polluted* at recyclable sites   or not.

When I spray Roundup pesticide   or plant mums against intruders,
flush unused pills   or return old meds to a hospital
pitch old paint buckets in the back-alley dumpster   or recycle house paint at
the dump
    I add to the 13 tons per second of world hazardous waste,
    40 million tons per year   or not.

2nd - Cliff Symay Rhodes: *The South*

The South be a held door
"thank you" and "no problem"
Balled in two head nods
The South be Good Morning and a smile
that fell in love with the fact you woke up
The South
be God willing and the creek don't rise
to the dreams
maturating into aspirations
The South be pork
as a seasoning
and love as a major food group
The South be fat
as a complement
and the correct measure for butter is
Yes
The South be NSU, FAMU, A&T
The South be Grambling, Morris Brown,
Tuskegee
The South be PHD Schoolin'
The South be grammatically correct
The South be high heat index
The South be understanding
humans ain't apex predators
when mosquitos hunt humans like hogs
The South be a family reunion
Big Mama's backyard
Spades, Bones, and Bid Whist
with a before dinner walk to the car
The South be moonshine
like great-granddaddy made to beat
prohibition
The South be calling your father daddy
without saying pause
The South be pause
Let's pray
The South be Thank God
Before your touch the food
The South be love

In a coin flip

The South rewrites history
No matter who won the war
The south be hard ER Nigger
With the same tongue that breathed Good
morning
The south be a minstrel show smile
head down holding doors
The south be pig scraps
slapped together
love and hot grease
was all the fixin's we could afford
The south be
hunting for the blood running through your
veins
The south be a spade digging up bones
beneath the family tree
The south be branches of our family tree
ending
strung up
from a family tree
The south be beer glasses
over
a sobering reality
The south be a false idol
The south be a half answered prayer
The south be a theology without a god
The south be birthplace
The south be resting place
The south be a hug from the parent
that abandoned you
The south be a deep sleep
That's undecided on being a dream or a
nightmare
God willing and the creek don't rise
The south be

1st - Bill Ayres: *We Share the World*

Flies crawl on the meat
   where the butcher hacks
and you show it   Jacob Lawrence

while my legs are stuck in the paint on your canvas
and my wings beat
           working to free me
                        I see this market around us
and I see the way you make it flat
                  filling your picture
                        with orange
 blue red black   with booths that stretch to the ocean
    people here to buy
             cloth   rugs baskets
you show us swarming   we're dots

    now I've freed myself from your painting
        I freckle the skin of the people
with my feet
     specks of orange

where I light on their arms, on their necks
               my friends halo the heads of people
who stroll, who dodge chickens children dogs
their sandals stepping
around puddles caca

                  thick in the air
we swarm what is damp   what is warm what is sticky   we're on
the melon
                the fish   now we're on the bowl of the man in front
          of your easel
                    he lifts the spoon to his mouth
we land on his cheek   we buzz in his ears

after Street to Mbari, by Jacob Lawrence, 1964
https://www.nga.gov/collection/art-object-page.79459.html

2nd - Aaliyah Anderson: *Today, You Will*

—after Lucille Clifton

look under my tongue —   for fruits gone

rotten.   Must I assure myself

he isn't my   boyfriend in sacrifice of

options? You always   trace like a

quick outline. I always   overhear a shrill

& say "it's pretty"   (to be better subjects than

you and me). *I can't convince you to not*

be religious, & you can't   *tell me I am.*

Yet, have you licked   the grass beneath

Adam, felt   magic   unfurl in your mucus?

You   bless me in unspoken words,

left me to harvest the wind   between your teeth. Fine.

Tomorrow,   I will bruise,   become my own

sedation.

1st - Eric Sundquist

walking meditation
the mountain
slowly

a cowbird's eggs
in the robin's nest
woodland sutra

nothing intersecting zen diagram

the stillness
of a singing bowl
morning star

2nd - Rebecca Lilly

shadows the same tone
no matter the leaf colors—
late afternoon cold

broken fishing line
hangs from a willow limb—
her incurable illness

brook freshets murmuring
out of cloud reflections . . .
I was younger then

my knife prunes the vines
without flowers yet—
there's the rest of my life

the long nights after she died—
I return to the river
in first light

A Note from Jim Kacian
about Contemporary Haiku

Jim Kacian is President of the American Haiku Foundation, and this year served as our haiku judge. Not only did he write personal responses to every writer who entered a poem in the category, he offered us at the Poetry Society this mini essay on what any writer intending to work in the field should know about the art of the haiku, as it is best practiced in contemporary English.

We all write out of the traditions with which we are familiar — how could it be otherwise? — and haiku is no exception. But few genres have had such a contorted transition from its culture of origin to its new home in English. Most of its difficulties arose quite early from simple misunderstandings, but they have been codified by subsequent misguided authority, which leaves us with the situation that currently exists.

The "popular conception" of what constitutes a haiku, as still taught in our education systems (when taught at all), and to be found widely promulgated on the internet, reinforces a simplistic and reductive model. It focuses primarily on syllable count, and conflates English-language syllables with Japanese *on*, which is demonstrably false and has been debunked for over a century. It also features an aspect practiced by only the most conservative elements of the genre — not even the Japanese write to this standard any longer. The result is poems that are, by comparison to classical Japanese originals and the best English-language models, overextended and flabby. But even more, this approach bypasses the more significant, if less overt, aspects of the genre: the juxtaposition of, and focus upon, images; the *kire* (cut) which divides these images; the asymmetrical positioning of these images; even the inclusion of a season word (*kigo*, though this is less a standard than it has been in previous centuries); all of which are far more central to the formulation of haiku in all languages than counting syllables.

What today would constitute a traditional approach to haiku in English among those experienced in the genre is a brief (8-12 syllable) poem in one to four, though usually one or three, lines, untitled (a title would be another line, and additional content), with a cut (a caesura that divides the poem into two, usually unequal, parts), and the pairing of (often nature-based) images. More innovative approaches may jettison one or more parts of this, but what remains in all instances is that a poem be brief, composed of images (rather than abstractions or exhortations), and focus on a moment of realization available to both author and reader. This is the standard employed in evaluating haiku by The Haiku Foundation (www.thehaikufoundation.org), the Haiku Society of America (https://www.hsa-haiku.org/), and by most other organizations who have made an advanced study of the genre. It is also the standard adopted by the Poetry Society of Virginia.

1st - Erin Newton Wells: *Incantation*

Week 1

First news of it. On page two. A line breached. A wood
full of legend, tales of those who whispered how
earth began, their feet in shadow, forest yet untouched.
A pine needle path. Oak mast. Shade. Abundance.
Enough for all. Their prophesies ignored.

The ranger advises we take care, the area not yet closed,
their hope to contain it. A few acres yet, hard to reach
in ravines dense with trees. Mind the smoke, he says,
direction of wind. We keep watch, a map on our
pocket-sized screen. A gray pall covers and consumes.

Peak season of leaves, inflamed now with sun, though
drought hit the region hard this year. Perfect tinder.

Week 2

Front page this time. Two thirds of it, at the top. Text,
with photos, continues on page two. The area now
is officially closed. Hikers and leaf-lookers turn back.

The containment area is widened, then breached again.
Flame, the nimble dancer, leaps with wind. Ash
smears fighters who rest on the ground. Their lungs
compose a story in carbon, like the layers of it in trees.

I mention what is less than thirty miles away in a forest
named for a trail made in dawn time, where feet
walked in reverence. No one in the group has heard of it.
I show them the screen, the map, the widening pall.
They look, then resume their talk of holiday shopping.

Week 3

Now, in its third week, it fills the front page and spills
to several more. Photos of a black streak, a gash seen
from above. Skeletons of animals and trees. Haze
appears at morning, over there, over sleeping houses,
coloring the sun in blood. I begin to wear a mask.

No one like us has died yet. But wings char. Hollows
where something slept do not look as they were.
Fern, laurel, trillium litter the air with burnt history.

Tonight, a moon strangely red-gold drifts by a chimney
next door and frames in silhouette, at the top, a seedling
of a large red-tip growing below, carried there by bird
or wind spreading whatever can be salvaged.

Week 4

For days I meant to tell them of the small tree. It will
break the bricks, reach down into the room
with branches, with leaves that look like flame, until
they cannot help but hear, each leaf the repetition,
the incantation, saying, *Let us live. Let us live.*

2nd - Deborah Baxter: *The Mountain Has a Fever*

In the village of Bondo, French Alps...

On my grasslands, dragonflies dart   in the air above the meadow,
and lupine grows in scattered   rainbows of purple, pink, and gold.
Winter snows melt as quickly as   ice in a champagne cocktail,
rivulets run down my sides like   sweat, moving stones, then boulders.

Deep within, where arctic ice   used to form,
my life's blood   drips away.
Mud, once forever frozen,   now thaws
letting loose ancient   earthworks as I fold
on myself, collapsing   in layers.
I rumble a warning,   but no one listens
until my village   is torn in two.

1st - Erin Newton Wells: *A Prayer for Broken Things*

A box stored in another box, in it a packet of tiny teeth,
under it another set, a careful note in each

with name and dates, years when the spirit of night
brought recompense beneath pillows, years

when a child might be lifted back to bed, brow smoothed,
soft words said in comfort for an injury

or dream. A small cast lies here, dingy white, sliced
on one side to let a mended wrist finally free,

a hole kindly fashioned for a thumb so someone hurt
and frightened might put it to her mouth

for consolation after she rolled from a bed and heard
bone crack. Here the ingenious splint,

a metal strip bent just so to keep the smallest finger still
while it healed, a piece of foam on which

it reclined, tiny chaise lounge, after the hand paused
too long in a door. All of this saved through all

these years because I hurt, too, when they were broken,
hurt now as they continue to walk into a world

that tries to break them, and sometimes does, my fists
clenched, but in prayer, to make them invincible.

2nd - Claudia Kessel: *Inversion*

He.

fears waking to blank mornings
the empty apartment
a white-clothed table set for one
the growl of silence, a crescendo
as the callous clock marks time like a metronome
for his body to breathe alone in rooms
where memories glare from picture frames
going months without touch—
only handshakes and jostled shoulders in crowds
watching the youthful world pass below
from his balcony, the mass of unknown bodies
commuting, eating, cursing, flirting, living their lives
indifferent to him, watering his begonias above them
the television's blare, a kind of desperation
for the missing voices, for the chaos of life
and ending his nights beneath cool sheets
un-warmed by the naked brown limbs
of a woman.

She.

suffers from too much presence
the mind aches for solitude
living in a house full of need
she is consumed daily, like bread
people need her hands to do things:
objects must be lifted, chopped, poured
cloth must be folded, water boiled in pots,
toilets unplugged

the voice desires to withdraw
but is always drawn out by her tongue
by gymnastics of inane conversation
the predictable things that must be said

she would give anything
to watch, unencumbered, the sunrise
to sit in her chair without moving her arms
making it to the bottom of her coffee cup, to its earthy black grounds
yearning for a day stretched out before her, free of tasks
mind withdrawn into symbol
to spend the afternoon swimming in watercolor
to picnic with God and the hummingbird
to float in the watery coolness of Bach's flute

instead her mind is pulled, reluctant, like a donkey
into the prosaic, the practical – the planning of meals
the commutes, the doctor's calls, the waking up and putting to bed

why can't she live for one day in the poem
she no longer desires youth, but craves old age
when for once, she might wake to an empty house
and fall to sleep under cool sheets.

1st - Peter LaBerge: *The Indisputable*

For Brad McGarry Bellaire, Ohio

Inside the house, above the basement
where D.J. bloodies Brad, there is
a white bowl of lemons sick with desire.

Watching this movie based loosely
on his life, I have to start there: sunlight

jeweling the canary fruit. Then, the afternoon
jeweling: an argument over a weed-eater.

Then, one man loving the other. And the other
staging a robbery of the house, chaotic as a
negative scratched to hell with a paperclip.

Across the state, four years earlier
& hours away, I lie
awake again on my grandfather's daybed.

I wait to jewel in the sun, scrolling through
neat rows of men on an app, notifications

                                  quiet, scrolling

through whole fields of men. The same way
years earlier, I believed
god scrolled through boys wherever I slept

to choose which ones won't walk home
from the next moon-stained pickup. The next

sunless barn, the next cherry-stained confession

After he's shot Brad,
D.J. drives to the closest lake,
scalps

the gun post-dusk. I never knew
Brad & now I never will, but I know this:

                              some houses

close their mouths while boys are still
dancing on their tongues. I watch D.J. pick up

his wife, then his daughter, then call the police.
His wife thumbs the god around her neck. *He was*
like a brother, D.J. says. *Robbery*. Below

the waterline, his daughter sits
on the front stoop, obedient in sunlight. At dusk,

god jams the sun back
into its socket. Pops a pill, falls asleep.

A group of women pool reward money
while stapling Brad's face to birch trees.

Is this really what god wants for us?

Is it?

2nd - Erin Newton Wells: *Thanksgiving at the Self-Checkout*

Shoppers with carts burdened for the holiday,
    coming soon, form a cue down the aisle
around displays, all sixteen stations occupied,
    so we wait, some with restless children,
and one with a comfort animal who yips
    as loudspeakers boom.

We inch forward, pause, inch forward.
    I am grateful for a turn at the small,
inadequate space and jam myself into it.

Next to me a woman stands frozen at her screen.
    It plays the jingly tune, *Help is on the way!*
Clearly, it is not. The employee in red apron
    circulates slowly among customers who
wait and fume at malfunctioning machines.
    I nod to my companion and say,

They should fix this. She shakes her head, says
    something in a language I do not know,
a sound of wind shushing over leaves.

I smile, as if to say, *yes, I agree.* Now the man
    on the other side of her joins in, his screen
also suddenly blocked so he cannot scan
    oranges he holds as an offering on the glass,
no help for him, either. He laughs and says
    something in yet another language,

the words quick, bright as an ocean sparkling
    on a shore, and I know the words vaguely
but not well, so he pantomimes it.

He pretends to give the machine a swift kick
    in the hardware. I laugh and do something
similar. At this, the woman thaws, her eyes alive.
    She shakes a finger at the naughty box,
speaks to it as we might to a misbehaving child.
    Others see the impromptu drama.

They loosen up, laugh, their children in hysterics
      at us, and the small animal is joyous.
Even Red Apron cracks a smile.

Each in turn, she waves her magic card to release
      our screens from bondage, and the lines
move toward holiday. I do not make this up,
      the little United Nations more or less usual
where I shop, help always somewhere on the way,
      and the loudspeakers unintelligible.

1st - Jerri Hardesty: *Heifer*

https://www.youtube.com/watch?v=gOHRGqAsqJ4&t=54s

It's time to stop the beauty madness!
I mean,
The other day,
I overheard a man call a woman
Heifer,
And so absurdly,
Poor, sweet little thing.
Wore a single-digit-sized wardrobe,
It was plain to see,
But some men
Are just impossible to please.
I think it's a social disease;
A recombinant virus
Of anorexic stereotypes
And airbrushed fantasies.
But my husband's tongue is always sweet,
So, if he ever said something like that
To me...
I'd just have to look for a deeper meaning.
On the surface,
It's easy as ABC:
Healthy, energetic, intelligent, fun, erotic, and real?
Well, yeah, I guess that's me.
Or maybe I'm
USDA Choice
Grade A Inspected
Hand Selected
Carefully Aged
All Natural
Organically Grown,
No additives, dyes, or preservatives.
From my prime rib
And sirloin tips
To my flank steak,
I'm 100% Pure woman
With melt-in-your-mouth sizzle.
Look into my ribeyes
And I'll New York strip for you,
Like they do in the Porterhouse

Over in Delmonico,
I'm something you can sink your teeth into!
My top round and bottom round
Are perfectly suited
To any recipe for which I'm recruited.
I'll be Filet Mignon every night,
Satisfy all your appetites.
So, when all those super models
Runnin' 'round on their little chicken legs
Just leave you wondering,
"Where's the beef?"
You bring your T-bone
Over here to my tenderloin,
Grab a couple of handfuls of rump roast,
And we'll ground round for a while,
Let stew all night in our own juices
Until we're well done —
Beef, it's what's for dinner!
You can grill me, thrill me,
Bake me, take me,
Boil me, broil me,
Skewer and stake me,
Roast and sauté me,
Stuff and filet me,
Fry me, try me,
Baste me, taste me,
Steam me, cream me,
Just don't waste me,
Mushroom-top and hollandaise me,
Burgundy and Beef Béarnaise me,
Barbecue me, you can even fondue me,
Because it's all good with you and me.
You make me want to say,
"Mooooooooooooooooooooooo, baby."
And you'll always be A-1 with me,
Because it just wouldn't be steak
Without the taste of A-1.
Yeah, it's that important.
But seriously, gentlemen,
Please,
Real women are not
Heifers.

Real women have real flesh
On real bones
With real curves
And real hearts
And real souls,
And if that's too much meat
On your menu,
On your plate,
I suggest you go vegetarian,
And learn to masturbate.

2nd - Terra Leigh: *Sake*

https://youtu.be/QGi9G0H1XaM?si=vZAjROqKUbFBEpJ5

I learned how to drink
Watching you down shots
Of sake.

I picked up my cup,
Tipped the source
Against my lips,

A slow twist
To this seal of self-control
I spent my life strengthening.

I hated the burn

But loved the way
It tasted against my
Naive tastebuds.

No other drinks held me
Like this one,

Like how you
Would pour me a glass
After work
And we would "Kanpai."

I always drank
My liquor
Slow,

Savoring this rebellion
Against myself.

The last drink we had
Was Chinese wine,
A sake substitute.

You joked about us
Becoming one.

And I, embarrassed,
Took two shots
And left for home
Tired.

I laid on the couch,
Knowing full well
You only looked at me
When I did something you wanted.

I was still so drunk
In my feelings

That I told you how I felt
A month later

And tumbled
In the stupor
Of your rejection.

I've been twisting the lid
On these sake bottles
Ever since.

I refuse to be
Red faced again.

CONTEST JUDGE BIOGRAPHIES

1923

2023

Laura Bylenok is the author of three books, including *Living Room* (University of Nebraska Press, 2022), winner of the Backwaters Prize in Poetry, *Warp* (Truman State University Press, 2015), winner of the T.S. Eliot Prize, and *a/0* (New Michigan Press, 2014). Her poetry has appeared in *Crazyhorse, Guernica, Ninth Letter, Arts & Letters, DIAGRAM*, and many other journals. She is an Associate Professor of English at the University of Mary Washington in Fredericksburg, Virginia.

Angela M. Carter is an author, poet, novelist, blogger, motivational speaker, spoken word performer, visual artist, and advocate/activist. She is the owner of 2nd Avenue Press (www.2ndavenuepress.com). She is the author of *Memory Chose a Woman's Body* (Unbound Content, 2014) and *Love is the Dying Dog* (forthcoming, mid 2024). Angela is a 2014 Pushcart Prize nominee, nominee for the 2015 Virginia Library Literary Award (poetry), and has been featured in a multitude of venues, including The KGB Club in Manhattan and Busboys and Poets. Her publications include *Silver Birch Press, Deep Water Literary Journal, Whurk, Vox Poetica, the Plath Poetry Project, Premiere Generation Ink, City Lit Rag, The Word Ocean, Worst Week Ever, Our Stories Untold, Gutsy Living,* and several anthologies. Contact: amhcarter@gmail.com

Barbara Crooker is author of twelve chapbooks and ten full-length books of poetry, including *Some Glad Morning*, Pitt Poetry Series, University of Pittsburgh Poetry Press, longlisted for the Julie Suk award from Jacar Press, *The Book of Kells*, which won the Best Poetry Book of 2019 Award from Poetry by the Sea, and *Slow Wreckage* (Grayson Books, 2024). Her other awards include Grammy Spoken Word Finalist, the WB Yeats Society of New York Award, the Thomas Merton Poetry of the Sacred Award, and three Pennsylvania Council fellowships in literature. Her work appears in literary journals and anthologies, including *The Bedford Introduction to Literature*.
www.barbaracrooker.com

Joanne Durham is the author of *To Drink from a Wider Bowl*, winner of the Sinclair Poetry Prize (Evening Street Press 2022) and *On Shifting Shoals* (Kelsay Books 2023). A 3-time Pushcart nominee, she won *Third Wednesday Magazine*'s 2023 Annual Poetry Contest and the Mary Ruffin Poole Prize from the NC Poetry Society. Her poems appear in *Poetry South, NC Literary Review, CALYX, Sky Island Journal* and many other journals and anthologies. She lives on the North Carolina coast, with the ocean as her backyard and muse. Visit her at https://www.joannedurham.com/

Roselyn Elliott is the author of four poetry chapbooks published by Finishing Line Press, and by State University of New York at Potsdam (winner of their Blueline Chapbook Award). Her poems and essays have appeared in *The Minnesota Review, New Letters, diode poetry journal, Streetlight Magazine, The Cumberland River Review, Hospital Drive*, and other publications. Rose holds an MFA from Virginia Commonwealth University and served as poetry editor at *Streetlight Magazine* 2017-

2019. She has taught writing at VCU, WriterHouse, PVCC and the Visual Art Center of Richmond. She lives in Richmond, VA.

Stan Galloway is the author and/or editor of 9 volumes of poetry, the founder of the Bridgewater International Poetry Festival and Pier-Glass Poetry, as well as a professor of English for more than 40 years.

Barry Gross has lived most of his life in Bucks County, PA, excluding two years across the Delaware River in Trenton, NJ, and seven years in Pittsburgh. His work has been in *The Mill Hunk Herald, The North Colorado Review, the Bucks County Playhouse Best of Talk Story*, and the *Classics Open Mic Anthology*. His books *Coiled Logic* (2015) and *Angled Portraits* (2017) were published by Red Dashboard LLC Press.

Pauletta Hansel's ten poetry collections include *Will There Also Be Singing?* (Shadelandhouse Modern Press, 2024); *Heartbreak Tree* (Madville Publications, 2022), which won the Poetry Society of Virginia's 2023 North American Book Award; and *Palindrome* (Dos Madres Press, 2017) winner of Berea College's Weatherford Award in Poetry. Her writing has been featured in *Cincinnati Review, Oxford American, Rattle, Appalachian Journal, Still: The Journal, Verse Daily* and *Poetry Daily*, among others. Pauletta was Cincinnati's first Poet Laureate and was 2022 Writer-in-Residence for The Public Library of Cincinnati and Hamilton County.

Henry Hart teaches English at the College of William and Mary. He has published four books of poetry and several books about modern poets. LSU Press will publish his book *Seamus Heaney's Gifts* in 2024.

Wendell Hawken earned her MFA from Warren Wilson College's Program for Writers. Hawken was recently named the inaugural Poet Laureate of Millwood VA, an unincorporated quirky village in the northern Shenandoah Valley where she lives on a grass farm with two dogs. The cat died.

Kim Hazelwood is the founder and poetry editor of *The Green Silk Journal*, online since 2005. She is the author of a poetry collection, *The Way You Just Shine* (2021) and *CoyoteBat!* (2011, 2021), a children's book. Currently she is crafting a second book of poetry. She greatly enjoys painting and playing music with her husband in their '70s folk rock duo and spending precious time with her granddaughter while living in the Shenandoah Valley.

Luisa Igloria, Poet Laureate of the Commonwealth of Virginia from 2020-2022, is the author of 14 books of poetry and 5 chapbooks, and is lead editor of *Dear Human at the Edge of Time: Poems on Climate Change in the U.S.* Recent national and international literary awards include the 2023 Immigrant Writing Series Prize from Black Lawrence Press; the 2019 Crab Orchard Open Competition Award for Poetry; the 2018 Center for the Book Arts Letterpress Chapbook Prize; the 2015

Resurgence Poetry Prize (the world's first major ecopoetry award); and the 2014 May Swenson Poetry Prize for *Ode to the Heart Smaller than a Pencil Eraser*.

Kirk Judd, founding member of West Virginia Writers, Inc., has lived, worked, trout fished and wandered around in West Virginia all his life. Kirk was a member of the Appalachian Literary League, a former president of West Virginia Writers, Inc., and is a founding member of and creative writing instructor for Allegheny Echoes, Inc., dedicated to the support and preservation of WV cultural heritage arts. Kirk is the author of three collections of poetry (*Field of Vision*, 1986, *Tao-Billy*, 1996, and *My People Was Music*, 2014) and is one of four well-known WV poets included in 2023's unique collaborative chapbook *Porch Poems*. He co-edited the widely acclaimed anthology *Wild, Sweet Notes – 50 Years of West Virginia Poetry 1950 –1999*. Kirk is internationally known for his performance work combining poetry and old-time music and has performed poetry in Ireland and across West Virginia, at fairs, concerts, and festivals, since the 1970s. He has been featured three times on American Public Radio on "The Poet and The Poem" with WV native Grace Cavalieri and has appeared on the acclaimed public radio show "Mountain Stage." Kirk was honored to be one of 5 readers selected for the installation ceremony of Louise McNeill Pease as WV Poet Laureate in 1979.

Jim Kacian is founder and president of The Haiku Foundation, founder and owner of Red Moon Press, editor-in-chief of *Haiku in English: The First Hundred Years*, and author of more than a score of books of haiku and other poetry. He lives in the Shenandoah Valley with his partner Maureen Gorman.

Sarah E N Kohrs is an artist and writer, with over 135 journal publications of her poetry and photography. She is the 2023 Peter K. Hixson Award in poetry winner and the 2022 Kingdoms in the Wild poetry award recipient for her chapbook, *Chameleon Sky*. Sarah has a teaching license, endorsed in Latin and Visual Arts, and homeschools, as well as works in her pottery studio, creating clay art to savor, and leading the rural non-profit Valley Educational Center for the Creative Arts. SENK lives in Shenandoah Valley, Virginia, kindling hope amidst asperity. http://senkohrs.com.

Stephanie Lask aka **Steph Love** is a spoken word artist, teacher, poetry slam and open mic host, web designer, and graphic designer. Originally from Virginia Beach, VA, she graduated in 2005 from Norfolk State University with a bachelor's in graphic design, and now resides in Norfolk, VA. She is the slammaster for the nationally ranked Verb Benders Slam Team, a teaching artist with Arts for Learning, the website administrator and on the board of directors for Southern Fried Poetry Slam, Inc., and co-host for the Rhythm & Wordplay open mic at Scandals Live. Stephanie is a hip hop junkie, a vinyl collector, and a cat lady, and has been a web and graphic designer for such regional and national non-profits and small businesses as Poet Fest, GROW Foundation, Southern Fried Poetry Slam, and The Watering Hole Poetry Retreat.

A founder of the Richmond, VA community River City Poets, **Joanna Lee** earned her MD from the Medical College of Virginia and a Master's in neuroscience from William & Mary. Her work has been published in *JAMA, Rattle, Fourth River* and elsewhere and has been nominated for both Pushcart and Best of the Net prizes. She is the author of the chapbook *Dissections* (2017) and a co-editor of the anthology *Lingering in the Margins* (2019); recently, she worked in collaboration with the Richmond Symphony to create "Letter to the City," which premiered at the Carpenter Theatre to sold out crowds in February 2024. She is also the current Richmond, Virginia Poet Laureate.

Margaret Mackinnon is the author of *The Invented Child*, winner of the Gerald Cable Book Award and the 2014 Literary Award in Poetry from the Library of Virginia. Her second book, *Afternoon in Cartago*, won the 2021 Richard Snyder Prize and has been published by Ashland Poetry Press. She lives in Richmond, Virginia, where she leads poetry workshops.

David Mills holds an MFA from Warren Wilson College and an MA from New York University. He has published four collections: *The Dream Detective, The Sudden Country, After Mistic*, and *Boneyarn*—the first book of poems about slavery in New York City and winner of the North American Book Award. His poems have appeared in *Ploughshares, Colorado Review, Crab Orchard Review, Jubilat, Callaloo, Obsidian, The Common, Brooklyn Rail, Rattapallax, The Literary Review, The African American Review, Poetry Daily, Evergreen Review* and *Fence*. He has received fellowships and grants from the New York Foundation for the Arts, Breadloaf, the Lannan Foundation, the Schomburg Center, the New York State Council on the Arts, *Cave Canem*, the Bronx Council on the Arts, Washington College, and the American Antiquarian Society, and he has won the Brooklyn non-fiction prize. A recipient of the Langston Hughes Society Award, he lived in Hughes's landmark Harlem home for three years and wrote the audio script for MacArthur-Genius-Award Winner Deborah Willis's curated exhibition *Reflections in Black: 100 Years of Black Photography*, which showed at the Whitney and Getty West Museums. The Juilliard School of Drama commissioned and produced a play by him. He has recorded his poetry on ESPN, RCA Records and has had poems displayed at the Venice Biennale and Germany's Documenta art exhibition.

Jay Paul's books are *The Latest Monument* and *Going Home in Floodtime*. He directs the Honors Program at Christopher Newport University and is always on the lookout for poetic liftoff.

Nathaniel Perry won the American Poetry Review/Honickman First Book Prize for his collection *Nine Acres*. He teaches at Hampden-Sydney College and edits the *Hampden-Sydney Poetry Review*.

Tully Potter was born in Edinburgh in 1942 but spent his formative years in South Africa. He is best known as a writer on classical music and an opera critic but has also published two poetry collections, *The Emigrant*, and *Night Ploughing and Other Poems*. His light verse books include 2021's *The Lockdown Poems, for six-to-eleven-year-olds of all ages*, and 2024's *Lockdown Poems, Volume Two*. Over the years he has given birth to hundreds of limericks, of greater or lesser scurrility.

Donald Wheelock's poems have appeared in *Able Muse, Blue Unicorn Ekphrasis, Rue Scribe, Think, Third Wednesday*, and many other journals welcoming formal poetry. His first full-length book of poems, *It's Hard Enough to Fly*, appeared in 2022 from Kelsay Books. David Robert Books published his second book, *With Nothing but a Nod*, in May of 2024.

Bart White is the author of two poetry collections, the Pushcart-nominated *The Faces We Had As Children* (FootHills Publishing, 2014) and *The Art of Restoration* (Jules Poetry Playhouse, Placitas, New Mexico, 2022). He is working on two books at present: forthcoming from FootHills Publications, *Your Session is About to Time Out*, a new collection of poems and prose written during a six-month stay in Oxford, and *Dear Lover, Soldier, Prisoner, Ghost: Poets Write across the Centuries*, an anthology of letter poems that is seeking a publisher.

Frederick Wilbur is a writer and architectural woodcarver living in the Blue Ridge Mountains of Virginia. His poetry collections are *As Pus Floats the Splinter Out* and *Conjugation of Perhaps*, and his work appears in many journals including *Appalachian Review, The Comstock Review, Hampden-Sydney Poetry Review, The Lyric*, and *Shenandoah*. Wilbur has authored many articles and three books on architectural and decorative woodcarving. *The Nelson County Garden Club: The First Fifty Years, 1935-1985* was recently underwritten by the local historical society. He is poetry co-editor and blogger for *Streetlight Magazine*. He was awarded the *Midwest Quarterly*'s Stephen Meats Poetry Prize for best poem of the year (2017).

Nicole Yurcaba is a Ukrainian American of Hutsul/Lemko origin. Her poems and reviews have appeared in *Appalachian Heritage, Atlanta Review, Seneca Review, New Eastern Europe*, and Ukraine's *Euromaidan Press, Lit Gazeta, Chytomo, Bukvoid*, and *The New Voice of Ukraine*. Nicole also serves as a guest book reviewer for *Sage Cigarettes, Tupelo Quarterly, Colorado Review*, and *Southern Review of Books*.

Kristin Camitta Zimet is the author of *Take in My Arms the Dark* and the editor of *The Sow's Ear Poetry Review*. Hundreds of her poems are in journals around the world. Her work has been performed in venues from concert hall to arboretum and has been featured in exhibitions on art/poetry.

CONTRIBUTOR BIOGRAPHIES
ADULT CONTESTS

1923

2023

Aaliyah Anderson (she/her) is an incoming freshman at the University of Mary Washington. She plans on double majoring in American Studies and English (Creative Writing). Her work appears in *Beaver Mag, BarBar, coalitionworks*, and elsewhere. Aaliyah's obsessed with burnt cheese and intersectional storytelling.

April J. Asbury teaches writing and literature at Radford University. She earned her M.F.A. from Spalding University and M.A. from Hollins. Her poetry and fiction appear in *Artemis Journal, Still: The Journal, Gyroscope Review*, and *The Anthology of Appalachian Writers. Woman with Crows*, her first collection, is available on apriljasbury.com.

Patsy Asuncion, a bi-racial, first-generation immigrant from inner-city Chicago, has two poetry books, *Cut on the Bias* and *Lineage of Weeds*, and poems in publications including *New York Times, About Place, Artemis* and *Cutthroat*. Patsy promotes diversity through national, community, local events (22,500+ YouTube views). See patasuncion.wixsite.com/patsy-asuncion, www.youtube.com/channel/UCiI15rIR04et_XYu70A_Hug

For most of his working life **Bill Ayres** has been a produce manager in the grocery store of dreams (he has worked in bookstores since the invention of paper). His poems have appeared in *Commonweal, Sojourners, The Windhover, river city, The Hollins Critic, Bird's Thumb, Sow's Ear....* His books are *What Passes for Wisdom* and *Jesus Poems*.

Deborah Baxter, an award-winning poet, has lived in the Tidewater area all her life. A graduate of Old Dominion University, she continues her studies at The Muse in Norfolk, Virginia. Her writing often reflects the quirks of Nature, as well as those of our own human hearts.

Elizabeth Black is a poet, painter, and printmaker. She has taught art classes at The George Washington University and Trinity University in Washington, D.C. and currently dedicates her life to poetry and painting. She participates in weekly poetry workshops and facilitates the regional haiku workshop, Towpath, associated with the American Haiku Society. She identifies her daily writing practice the past 45 years as her therapy, joy, and sometimes, frustration.

Renaissance woman, **Laura J. Bobrow** has achieved professional status in multiple careers: painter, sculptor, songwriter, folksinger, author, and poet. Her poems have appeared in various media as far away as Abu Dhabi. Her short stories have appeared in numerous anthologies. She is, in addition, and perhaps foremost, an acclaimed professional storyteller.

A native Virginian, **Wes Carrington** turned to poetry at some point in junior high school as a shorter alternative to meet his English teachers' weekly writing requirements and grew to love it while later living and working abroad. He is just starting to appear here and there.

Dr. Kathleen P. Decker is a Past President of the National League of American Pen Women, Seattle Branch, and is Past Vice President of the Poetry Society of Virginia. Her books of poetry include *Russian Reverie, Whispers on Paper, Essence of Woman, Updraft*, and *Fishmas*. Poetry anthologies she has edited include *My Neighbor's Life, On Crimson Wings, Quilted Poems, Views of Virginia*, and *Blended Voices*.

Alongside her poetry book Apocryphal (San Francisco Press), **Anna Evas** is published in literary journals such as *Michigan Quarterly Review, THINK, Worcester Review*, and *Long Poem Magazine* (UK). She is a recording pianist and an award-winning composer of concert level, contemporary classical music.

Rich Follett, the Poet Laureate of Strasburg, VA, has authored *Responsorials* (with Constance Stadler, 2009), *Silence, Inhabited* (2011), *Human &c.* (2013), and *Geminations* (with Constance Stadler, 2023) through NeoPoesis Press, and *Photo-Ku* (2016) through NightWing Publications. Rich is featured in the ODU Virginia Poets Database at https://digitalcommons.odu.edu/virginiapoets. Information and publications at www.richfollett.com

Eric Forsbergh, a Vietnam veteran, earned in 2022 a master's certificate at a majority-minority seminary (John Leland Institute). With over 100 poems published, he has won the Poe prize twice. His second book *This Mortal Coil*, on the subject of DNA and its consequences, was published in October, 2023.

Anna Isabella Fratarcangelo is a junior literary arts major at Appomattox Regional Governor's School. She has received three Silver Keys and one Gold Key in poetry from the Scholastic Art & Writing Awards, placed 2nd in the VHSL Nonfiction Contest, been a member of the VHSL State Writing Champion Team, held the title of National Youth Correspondent, and served as the managing editor of her school's yearbook *The Flame*. She is honored to be given a platform to share her voice.

In addition to this and prior PSV collections, **Greg Friedmann**'s poetry has appeared in the *Sky Island Journal, The Northern Virginia Review, The Maryland Literary Review, Panoplyzine, Beyond Words*, and other journals. He and his wife live alongside a channel of the Potomac River in northern Virginia, inspiring him to write on riparian themes, particularly on nature's power to console and inspire. **Mark Fryburg** moved from journalism, public relations and flight instruction to poetry just two years ago. This year, aged 73, he gained the PSV win, a national journal placement, and a national contest Honorable Mention. This Oregon native and Stanford grad retired in Botetourt County, with bride Laura, and two pups.

Gail Giewont chairs the Literary Arts department at Appomattox Regional Governor's School. Her poetry chapbook, *Vulture*, is available from Finishing Line Press. She has won the Shann Palmer Poetry Prize, the Many Mountains Moving Poetry Prize, and the Fralin Museum's Writer's Eye Poetry Prize, among others. She lives in North Chesterfield, VA, with her rescue beagles, Bob Barker, Bee, and Mrs. Waddlesworth.

June Goodenough, aka **Ricci**, has been published in small press poetry anthologies, military base papers, and *The Alcona County Review*. She earned an English B.A. and is an Air Force retiree, an equestrian, a Black Belt, and, as a recurve archer, has shot a bullseye 'Robin Hood' at 50 yards.

Jerri Hardesty lives in the woods of Alabama with husband, Kirk, who is also a writer. They run the nonprofit poetry organization, New Dawn Unlimited, Inc. (NewDawnUnlimited.com) Jerri has had over 600 poems published and has won more than 2200 awards and titles in both written and spoken word poetry.

Wendell Hawken (she/her) earned her MFA from Warren Wilson College's Program for Writers. Publications include four chapbooks and five full collections. Hawken serves as the inaugural Poet Laureate of Millwood VA, an unincorporated quirky village in the northern Shenandoah Valley where she lives.

A. Logan Hill is a poet, writer, artist, and educator based in Richmond, Virginia. He has an MFA in Poetry from UMASS Amherst, a B.A. in English from James Madison University, and spent his formative years at The American Boychoir, where he graduated in 2004. When not teaching, he types poetry on demand using a 1953 Royal Quiet Deluxe typewriter.

You can read **Ken Hines**' poems in *Rust & Moth, Dunes Review, Burningword Journal* and other literary magazines. You'll find his essays in *The Millions* and *Philosophy Now*. A recent Pushcart Prize and Best of the Net nominee, he lives in monument-free Richmond, Virginia with his wife Fran.

Jim Huneycutt's B.A. at Randolph-Macon College came in 1983; his master's certificate from The Naropa Institute arrived in 1985. Recent publications include a foreword to Edgar Tiffany's "Audie Murphy in Saigon." His villanelle "War is the Greatest Con Ever Devised," appeared in the March 2024 edition of *The Mid-Atlantic Review*.

Poet/teacher **Donna Isaac**, ever a Virginian, works with Minnesota community writing. She has published four poetry books/chapbooks with a new book, *In the Tilling*, forthcoming (Finishing Line Press), 2025. She lives on a pond that houses two giant snappers, herons, and other wildlife. <donnaisaacpoet.com>

Joseph M. Jablonski is the typewriting street poet of Winchester, Virginia. As the "Walking Mall Poet," he writes personalized poems for passersby on antique typewriters. In addition to recently being published by Livina Press, he is an artist-in-residence currently at the Peter Bullough Foundation and The Good Listening Project.

Claudia Kessel works as a nonprofit grant writer in Williamsburg, Virginia. Her poetry has been published in *Richmond* magazine as a finalist in the 2021 Shann Palmer Poetry Contest, issued by James River Writers, and in print and online literary journals *Uppagus* and *Lullwater Review*.

Sarah E N Kohrs has poetry published in *Arboreal Literary Magazine, Bluebird Word, Chariot Press, Culinary Origami, The Elevation, GROUND, Kitchen Quarterly Review, Louisiana Literature, Stoneboat, Wild Roof Journal,* and numerous other journals. SENK lives in Shenandoah County, Virginia, kindling hope amidst asperity. Find out more at http://senkohrs.com.

Peter LaBerge is the author of the chapbooks *Makeshift Cathedral* (YesYes Books) and *Hook* (Sibling Rivalry Press). His poetry has received a Pushcart Prize and has appeared in *AGNI, American Poetry Review, Best New Poets, Kenyon Review, New England Review, Pleiades,* and *Tin House,* among others. Peter received his MFA from New York University. He is the founder and editor-in-chief of *The Adroit Journal* and lives online at peterlaberge.com.

Rebecca Lilly has published haiku widely. Of her several collections of haiku, her most recent is *Aporia* (2021, Red Moon Press).

Christina Linsin is a poet and teacher in Virginia. Her work examines connections with nature, complexities of mental illness, and difficulties creating meaningful connections with others amid life's obstacles. Her poems have been published in *Still: The Journal, Stone Circle Review, Tinderbox Poetry Journal, The Mid-Atlantic Review,* and others.

Amasa Maleski is a poet from Arlington, VA studying engineering at the University of Virginia. He is an alum of the 2020 DC Youth Slam Team and was Arlington's inaugural Youth Poet Laureate. During his tenure & beyond, Amasa has led many creative writing workshops throughout local libraries and schools.

Cliff Symay Rhodes is a poet, editor, musician and educator from Norfolk, Virginia. He is an accomplished poetry slam winner and the host of the Monday Night Open Mic at historic The Venue on 35th also in Norfolk, VA. His book *Poetry is like Medicine* is available online.

Hannah Rouse is a senior Literary Arts major at Appomattox Regional Governor's School. She has been published in *Asgard, Fledge, Under the Madness, Appelley, Free Spirit, Currents,* and *You Might Need to Hear This.* She's placed nationally in 21 writing contests and received first prize for the Sarah Mook Poetry Contest in 2023. Hannah is also a competitive dancer who enjoys spending time with her two cats and dog.

Felicity Sheehy's *Losing the Farm* won the Munster Literature Centre's international chapbook prize. Her poems have appeared in *The New Republic, The Southern Review, The Irish Times, The Yale Review, Poetry Daily, Poetry Northwest, Prairie Schooner, P.N. Review, The Adroit Journal, Colorado Review, Alaska Quarterly Review, 32 Poems, Shenandoah, Blackbird,* and elsewhere. She was recently listed as one of *Narrative Magazine's* 30 below 30 emerging writers.

Elizabeth Spencer Spragins has written for more than 100 journals and anthologies in 11 countries. She is the author of three original poetry collections: *Waltzing with Water* and *With No Bridle for the Breeze* (Shanti Arts Publishing) and *The Language of Bones* (Kelsay Books). elizabethspencerspragins.wordpress.com.

Richard Stimac has published a poetry book *Bricolage* (Spartan Press), two poetry chapbooks, and one flash fiction chapbook. In his work, Richard explores time and memory through the landscape and humanscape of the St. Louis region.

Eric Sundquist, a former teacher and scholar, lives in the woods near Batesville, Virginia.

The biology student finding ways to describe experiments for class assignments was **toni tyler** weaving tales or writing poetry. Fruitful careers in cytogenetics research and public service then retirement offered a return to her 1st Love of storytelling and poetry. "Only minor awards, only published in two Anthologies, but I keep putting pen to pad."

Terra Leigh (Walker) is a poet and editor from Chesapeake, Virginia. She is the winner of the 2013 Steger Poetry Prize from Virginia Tech, where she received a BA in English/creative writing. She earned her MFA in poetry from Drew University. Her poetry collections include *Ignite* (2018), *So Far Away* (2019), and *The Girl on the Swings: Transparency* (2022).

Erin Newton Wells is a teacher, artist, and writer, currently living in Charlottesville, Virginia, where she is content to observe the world and write about it.

ACKNOWLEDGMENTS

The 2024 Poetry Society of Virginia Contest Committee consisted of Guy Terrell, Derek Kannemeyer, and John Berry (adult contests) and Cathy Hailey (student contests) with oversight from the society president Cherryl Cooley.

The anthology of the 2024 Contest Winning Poems was edited by Derek Kannemeyer and published by High Tide Publications, Inc..

The cover art is by Terry Cox-Joseph.

www.ingramcontent.com/pod-product-compliance
Lightning Source LLC
Chambersburg PA
CBHW072038170626
46811CB00008B/3099